azaleas

WEATHERHEAD BOOKS ON ASIA

azaleas

A BOOK OF POEMS

KIM SOWŎL

Translated, with an introduction, by
DAVID R. McCANN

COLUMBIA UNIVERSITY PRESS NEW YORK

This publication has been supported by the Richard W. Weatherhead Publication Fund of the East Asian Institute, Columbia University.

This book is published with the support of the Sunshik Min Endowment for the Advancement of Korean Literature, Korea Institute, Harvard University.

COLUMBIA UNIVERSITY PRESS
Publishers Since 1893
NEW YORK CHICHESTER, WEST SUSSEX

Library of Congress Cataloging-in-Publication Data
Kim, Sowŏl, 1903–1934.
    [Chindallekkot. English]
    Azaleas : a book of poems / Kim Sowŏl ; translated, with an introduction, by
David R. McCann.
        p. cm. — (Weatherhead books on Asia)
    ISBN 978-0-231-13973-1

    1. Kim, Sowŏl, 1903–1934—Translations into English.   I. McCann, David R.
(David Richard), 1944–   II. Title.   III. Series.
PL991.415.C5C513   2007
895.7'13—dc22
                                                            2006029591

Columbia University Press books are printed on permanent and
durable acid-free paper.
Designed by Chang Jae Lee
Printed in the United States of America

Fleurs de la Montagne

Fleurs sur la montagne fleurissent,
Les fleurs fleurissent.
Automne, printemps, été jusqu'à la fin
Les fleurs fleurissent.

Haut sur la montagne,
Là-haut sur la montagne
Les fleurs sont fleurissantes
Si éloignées, si loin.

Un petit oiseau
Haut sur la montagne chante.
Ami des fleurs,
Sur la montagne il demeure.

Fleurs sur la montagne
Tombent, fleurs se laissent tomber.
Printemps, été, automne jusqu'à la fin
Les fleurs tombent.

Translation of "Flowers of the Mountain" in loving memory of
Helen Louise Summer McCann (1917–2006)
by her husband, Richard V. E. McCann

CONTENTS

ACKNOWLEDGMENTS

I have used primarily two sources for the translations in this collection: Kim Yongjik's *Kim Sowŏl chŏnjip (Complete Works of Kim Sowŏl)*, published by Seoul National University Press in 2001, and an unpublished edition by my friend and colleague Professor Kwŏn Yŏngmin. I am grateful for Kwŏn Yŏngmin's advice, learning, and friendship over the years, as I am to so many others, from riders met on trains between Andong and Seoul in the 1960s to students, colleagues, and others who have not only endured my questions and my enthusiasm about Sowŏl, his poetry, and his times, but also provided information and encouragement.

I wish to formally express my gratitude for a translation grant from the International Communication Foundation, which helped me keep going with the project during a difficult passage. I was able to explore some of the ideas for the introduction at the University of California at Berkeley in presenting the 2004 Tompkins Lecture, and at the University of Washington that same year in the Andrew W. Markus Lecture; I am deeply grateful for the opportunity and the response. My special thanks to Professor Jiwon Shin at the University of California and Professor Scott Swaner at the University of Washington. My thanks also to Young-Jun Lee and to Jung Ja Choi for their patient help with the manuscript and for their suggestions about ways to improve it.

My deepest thanks go to my wife, Ann, who was there in Korea at the beginning of this project and with me ever since.

azaleas

INTRODUCTION

SOWŎL'S POETRY AND PLACE
IN KOREAN LITERATURE

Kim Chŏngsik, known by the sobriquet Sowŏl (White Moon), lived for only thirty-two years (1902–1934) and published but one book of poems, *Azaleas* (*Chindallaekkot*, 1925), yet he became one of twentieth-century Korea's most beloved and well-known poets. Editions of his collected poems have been published in great numbers, especially during the 1960s and 1970s, when his works were made part of the middle- and high-school curricula, at least in South Korea. During the 1980s, a period of intense focus in literary and intellectual circles on the social and political role of the writer, Sowŏl was criticized for having failed to engage the social and political issues of his day, notably including the complex nexus of the Japanese colonial occupation of Korea (1910–1945). A more balanced view of his life and work has emerged since the 1980s, which takes special note of his extraordinary control of the expressive capabilities of the Korean language in his works; his deft appropriation of folk-song images, tonalities, and rhythmic forms; and his still elusive qualities as an early Korean modernist poet.

Sowŏl's popular following remains strong. In 2002, when *Siin segye* (*Poet's World*) conducted a readers' poll to identify Korea's favorite poets of the past one hundred years, Sowŏl topped the list. Sowŏl's best-known poem, "Azaleas," has appeared over the years in several song versions, and in 2002 it was performed by the Korean rock group Novasonic on their compact disc *Remastering*. In 2003, the singer Maya included her own version on *Born to Do It*.

The greater part of Korean scholarship and critical writing on Sowŏl has tended to focus on the ten or dozen of his poems most widely known through their presentation in Korean textbooks. They are wonderful poems, to be sure; but *Azaleas* as a whole is left standing more as a monument, the place where the original versions of the well-known poems are interred, than as a book to be read in its entirety. Among other things, this has meant that any given poem is not read against other poems, while the entire collection is not read as a work in its own right. This abbreviated reading practice may account, in turn, for the persistence of the summary assessment of Sowŏl as a folk-song poet, focusing as it does on the poems that fit the characterization while ignoring the labor as well as the varied materials of the remaining hundred or more poems that constitute the book.

Azaleas is a big collection of poems. In customary practice, a book of poems might contain forty or perhaps fifty pieces. This does not mean that larger numbers of poems or lines make a poem project great. T. S. Eliot's *The Wasteland*, to which Eliot added an extensive notes section so that the publisher would consider it worth doing as a book, was still shorter than twenty pages.[1] But there are 127 poems in *Azaleas*, arranged in sixteen discrete sections. One, "The Cricket," contains nineteen poems, twelve of which are of four lines or fewer. The three poems in "Summer's Moon," though, are forty-eight, twenty-four, and thirty-two lines in length. Thematic arrangements also seem to be at play, with, for example, recurrent sequences of disturbing dream images, or the death images in the section "Alone" leading to the extraordinary "Invocation," one of Sowŏl's best-known works. The "Azaleas" section is its own tour de force, in three dimensions: it contains several of the best known of Sowŏl's works and most famous of all twentieth-century Korean poems, "Road Away," "Wangsimni," "Azaleas," "Sakchu Kusŏng," "Cuckoo," and "Flowers of the Mountain"; it moves within a controlled environment from one poem to the next; and it argues, by its clearly palpable structuring, for an alertness, in reading the other poems in the book, to the overall structure, argument, and plot of the whole.

Azaleas tells a story. A series of juxtaposed images and an array of voices combine to bring a young Korean writer from the more northern, P'yŏngyang area into the modern literary world of Seoul, the cosmopolitan capital of Korea. What he did when he left the north, then while he stayed in or around Seoul for two years as a student and writer, and under what terms he left it to return to the north constitute the story of this book, one that has always seemed to me to deserve to be encountered as a whole.

What will today's reader make of it? I find a close literary resemblance to Rimbaud and his "Le bateau ivre," that long, brilliant poem about throwing loose the lines and sailing down the river and away; but also a biographical mirroring between two poets who wrote youthfully and brilliantly, then gave it all up and walked off, Rimbaud to Africa and his series of failed business enterprises and collapsing health, Sowŏl back to the region near P'yŏngyang that he had left earlier, to a job as a regional newspaper distributor and a life descending into depression, drink, and an early death, perhaps deliberate, from an overdose of opium.

What story will readers find in this English-language version of *Azaleas*? Whatever that turns out to be, by encountering the entire work in English outside the Korean national narratives of any particular poem's meaning, readers will have made something entirely new of Sowŏl and his work: a writer of the twenty-first-century literary world.

Kim Kijin, a leader of the Korean Artists Proletarian Federation (KAPF) in the 1920s and 1930s, wrote of Sowŏl's poetry that there was little to recommend it beyond a certain charm of expression in the folk-song style.[2] For Kim Kijin, any poet not fully committed to KAPF's programmatic and didactic goals had significance only for examples of the sorts of literary work that Korean readers should avoid. Published in *Kaebyŏk* (*Creation*), the leading literary and intellectual journal of the day, where Sowŏl, as it happened, had also published many of his poems, Kim Kijin's critique is historically bound to the period of the 1920s in Korea, yet it stubbornly persists as a lingering critical gesture. *A History of Korean Literature*, published in 2003, states the charge as follows: "Kim [Sowŏl] . . . seldom took firm hold of contemporary life."[3] A study of the North Korean literary reception of Sowŏl offers a variation on this theme. *P'yŏngyang e p'in chindallaekkot* (*An Azalea That Bloomed in P'yŏngyang*), a gathering of North Korean responses to Sowŏl and his work, notes the overly personal, bourgeois sentimentality of the poems, contrasting it with a more public, Korean nationalist sentiment.[4]

I was forcefully reminded of the official assessment in the Democratic People's Republic of Korea of Sowŏl's limits as a poet when a government guide, named Kim Chŏngsik—coincidentally, Sowŏl's full name—repeatedly, though in the main good-naturedly, hectored me in the course of a week-long visit to P'yŏngyang, Hamhŭng, and Wŏnsan about my professed interest in Sowŏl's work. Doubly ironic, then, was my discovery of the scene in a North Korean television drama series about KAPF in which two of the lead characters stand on the shore of a lake while one, the man, gravely recites the refrain from Sowŏl's poem "Cuckoo" (Chŏpdongsae): "Chŏp-dong, chŏpdong, a'uraebi chŏpdong . . ."[5]

Korean literary history has shown a similar disposition toward reducing Sowŏl's work to its simplest components. *A History of Korean Literature* characterizes Sowŏl's appeal in the following terms:

> little specificity of plot. . . . Images [that] are commonplace, and . . . used to exploit stock responses. The poems offer conventional feelings about the sorrow of love, and this calculated indeterminacy, a characteristic of folk song, contributes to their popularity. . . . Simple diction, subtle versification, repetition with special effects, economy—all contribute to their charm.[6]

In his "Remembrance of Sowŏl" (Sowŏl ŭi ch'uŏk),[7] Sowŏl's teacher and mentor Kim Ŏk seemed eager to explain that his former student and literary disciple had been a much better folk-song poet than modernist poet, perhaps, or KAPF writer.

Kim Ŏk wrote that Sowŏl's other poems lacked the "youthful brightness" of his work in the folk-song style. The editors of *Kaebyŏk*—perhaps none other than Kim Ŏk himself—had inserted the label "folk-song poem" on the page where Sowŏl's "Azaleas" first appeared,[8] but for whose benefit, for what purpose? Was it meant to locate the poem in a certain segment of the literary marketplace? Kim Ŏk and others were publishing folk-song poems at the time, so perhaps the gesture in Sowŏl's case was intended as an acknowledgment that here was a *real* folk-song poem. Kim Ŏk mentioned "Azaleas" in the "Remembrance" as one of Sowŏl's works that every reader would be familiar with. The labeling also seems resonant with the argument at the time, in the early 1920s, over various types of literature and their social or aesthetic purposes, so it may have been intended as a rejoinder of sorts to KAPF's program of socialist realism. In other words, Kim Ŏk may well have been viewing and using Sowŏl as a positive example of the sort of literary product he was advocating, as opposed to Kim Kijin's use of Sowŏl as an example of what not to do as a writer.

Kim Ŏk mentions in the "Remembrance" that, as a poet, Sowŏl hated being called a folk-song poet, even though, he went on to say, folk-song poetry was Sowŏl's true métier. Perhaps thinking of Kim Kijin's dismissive comment, Sowŏl may indeed have felt some special bitterness in the last years of his life because of his failure to make a living as a writer. Kim Ŏk also mentions Sowŏl's businesslike approach to life, observing that he "did not shy away from calculating his own interests in any given situation," while noting that his uncompromising determination led at times to "disappointments that others might have borne gently, [but that] he encountered with a bitter sadness."

The "Remembrance" comments at length on the poem "Road Away" as an example of Sowŏl's efforts to revise, to work and rework a poem. According to Kim Ŏk, "Road Away" constitutes a true landmark in its deliberate disassembly of the traditional Korean verse line and reassembly of it for printing on a page for reading. Ironically, this is the poem that Kim Kijin cited also in his critical reference to Sowŏl, perhaps because he imagined that such poems came easily or naturally to "folk-song poets." As Sowŏl's teacher at the Osan Middle School and the Paejae Academy, and after, as Sowŏl's literary mentor, Kim Ŏk knew firsthand, and attempted to demonstrate to the readers of the *Chosŏn chungang ilbo* (*Chosŏn Daily News*) in 1935, just how demanding was the work in making a folk-song poem.

Kim Ŏk's poignant essay on Sowŏl is now part of a remarkable range of work on the poet, amounting to several hundred separate articles and books, including many different editions of his poems. One can trace through a listing of these works—for example, in Kim Yongjik's *Kim Sowŏl chŏnjip* (*Complete Works of Kim Sowŏl*)—the shifting critical discourse, from the poet Sŏ Chŏngju's 1959 essay on resentful feeling in Sowŏl's poetry to the essays from the 1970s on the then new subject of *han* (resentment) and Sowŏl's poetry, a quite different reading based on the concept of *han* as a signifier of Korean national culture.[9] A history of Korean literary criticism can be read in the titles of all these various works seeking to articulate their authors' engagements, at many different levels and for many different purposes, from professional to political to personal, with the works of the simple folk-song poet Kim Sowŏl. What accounts for such sustained interest? Why have so many critics, poets, and literary historians spent so much time and energy trying to make an account of Kim Sowŏl's poetry? One reason is obvious: it has been a key part of the secondary-school and college curricula in Korea for many decades, and it is eminently sensible to try to have something to say, as a professional writer, about any phenomenon that is well known to a large number of people.

Gazing from the outside, from a culture lacking national totemic figures, peering in at Korea's literary world, where a best-selling book of poetry may sell 500,000 or more copies, I shall venture a few observations as a guide for other readers. A huge amount has been written and published about a relatively small number of poems. What has been written and published about Sowŏl has changed, over time, and reflects changes in analytical method, terms and concepts, political culture, the spoken and written Korean language, as well as such other matters as simple and unrelenting generational succession. Yet, however shaped or nuanced by anticolonial imperatives, national curriculum requirements, or other, more recent historical circumstances, the literary critical-historical readings of Sowŏl's poetry, and, in particular, of the relatively small number of his more than 250 works that became a fixed part of school curricula, seem reductionist: Sowŏl wrote charming poems, but they lack reference to modern urban life, entertain no direct engagement with Korea's colonized situation, and deploy no unconventional imagery or language, or nothing but conventionalized, folk-song-style imagery and diction.

Given space, however, which among other things means simply liberation from such critical imperatives, the poems themselves make their own rejoinder. "Azaleas," for example, can be read as a love song, an anticolonialist spell, and a poem about itself being read as a poem.

What kind of a poet was Sowŏl? How might he have explained what he set out to do in his work as a poet? I should like to propose allowing him to bring these reflections to a close. Precisely because his works have become so thickly bound with critical readings of all sorts, I turn to consider one of his unpublished and therefore unknown and unbound poems, now available thanks to new editions of Sowŏl's writings. The poem is "Rainy Day" (Pi onŭn nal):[10]

A rainy day. Some previous day, I might have recited
Verlaine's song, how the rain of tears falls
in my heart, but
a rainy day, today,
and I just say, "It's raining."
Rainy day, today, the poplar leaves are green,
a flock of sparrows perches chattering
in the shadows of the leaves,
a frog, a big fellow sitting on a leaf, lets go a croak
and leaps into the ditch.
A fine rain, the drops trembling,

one, then two joining, running down.
Even the rain falling in P'yŏngyang's Changbyŏlli
is all the same old rain, but different
from an earlier day's. Asleep on the warm part
of the floor, my little one stretches
and wakes up with a cry. I say to her
"Look, see how it's raining,"
as I lift her up, my child
just two years old this year,
holding her close to me.

"Rainy Day" begins with a reference to Paul Verlaine's "Il pleure dans mon cœur," muses playfully on the line and the image, then concludes with a quite plain, direct, human gesture. The reference to the two-year-old child suggests that the poem was written around 1921 or shortly after, two years after Sowŏl's first child, his daughter Kusaeng, was born. There is no indication of youthful awe, on Sowŏl's part, at the literary company he claims to keep, nothing other than equal comfort with that literary reference, the place, P'yŏngyang, the rain, and the young child looking out the window.

The poem's opening lines present a subversive gesture with the acknowledgment, as if it said, "Ah yes, Verlaine, the French poet, wrote about a day like this. Raining in the heart, raining on the town. And were I in a mood literary, I certainly could have deployed that French poet, because I (and you, Dear Reader) know French poetry, do we not?" Even as he cites the foreign poet, however, Sowŏl is already moving away from any sort of homage, using the word "song" (*norae*) rather than "poem" (*si*) to state its genre. But then again, is that not what Verlaine's poem actually is? No homage, then; it is raining. Readers familiar with Verlaine would also know "Chanson d'automne," a true *paysage triste*, and might associate the scene with the autumn.

"Rainy Day" suggests that Sowŏl was engaged but not overwhelmed by the poetry of the Continental Symbolists. A selection of Verlaine's poems, translated into English by the British poet Arthur Symons[11] and translated, in turn, into Korean by Kim Ŏk, was included in *Onoe ŭi mudo* (*The Dance of Anguish*) in 1921.[12] In his "Remembrance of Sowŏl," Kim Ŏk noted the enthusiasms in the early 1920s about every foreign literary fashion. "Rainy Day" might show that enthusiasm, as did Sowŏl's essay "Sihon" (The Soul of Poetry),[13] in which he quoted in English two verses of one of Symons's poems, but Sowŏl's engagement seems measured and deliberate. It might be suggested, then, that the so-called folk-song poet was in fact the product of Sowŏl's deliberate choice to do the work necessary to construct a poetical identity, language, set of images, and array of responses that he, and no doubt Kim Ŏk as well, believed would find a ready response among readers of the time.

The life of Amedeo Modigliani provides an instructive parallel from the field of art history. Modigliani is generally—but also professionally in the field of art history—taken as an epitome of the Bohemian: given to alcohol, addicted to hashish, involved with too many women, creator of a distinctive but easy to dismiss style "based" on African folk art, and dead before the age of forty.[14] One could add that Modigliani moved from an important but peripheral geographical location, Livorno, Italy, to the center of the European artistic realm, Paris, just as Sowŏl moved for a time from the countryside near P'yŏngyang, the capital of "more muscle and more brains," to Seoul.[15]

Modigliani created only two or three landscape paintings, direct representations of the world around him; he focused instead on portraits of residents of Paris, both those inside the artistic and intellectual circles as well as outsiders. In Korean literary history, especially from the 1980s with its summoning of all Korean artists to account, Sowŏl has been seen as having failed to represent the modern urban scene and its inhabitants in his work. This was a point my North Korean guide made repeatedly. But Modigliani worked to develop the distinctive visual line, no doubt borrowed from African folk art, through which his portraits of the Parisian demimonde took their shape, while Sowŏl labored at making a distinctive voice speak through the rhythmic lines of his poems. Kim Ŏk's

"Remembrance" reminds us repeatedly about the work involved, in Sowŏl's case, as do the different, changing versions of his poems as published in literary journals, especially *Kaebyŏk*, prior to their appearance in *Azaleas* in 1925.

Several generations of Korean readers have read and memorized Sowŏl's poems. Literary critics and historians have provided their accounts. Several of the poems have become popular songs, while over the years, a number of translators have presented their own engagements with them.

My own involvement with Sowŏl's work, in the company of many Korean and other admirers of it, began in 1966, when I discovered a book of Sowŏl's poems[16] translated by Kim Dong Sung and started reading and then trying my own hand at translating them. My part in this task ends here in Watertown in 2006, at least for the moment. It is my hope that the work will continue as other readers find Sowŏl's example worth emulating, his labor rewarded by their own.

Notes

1. T. S. Eliot, *The Annotated Waste Land with Eliot's Contemporary Prose*, ed. Laurence Rainey (New Haven, Conn.: Yale University Press, 2005), p. 25.

2. Kim Kijin, "Hyŏnsidan ŭi siin" [The Poets of Today's Poetic World], *Kaebyŏk* [*Creation*], April 1925, pp. 29–30.

3. Peter H. Lee, "Early Twentieth-Century Poetry," in Peter H. Lee, ed., *A History of Korean Literature* (Cambridge: Cambridge University Press, 2003), p. 353.

4. Kwŏn Yŏngmin, ed., *P'yŏngyang e p'in chindallaekkot* [*An Azalea That Bloomed in P'yŏngyang*] (Seoul: T'ongil Munhak, 2002), p. 33.

5. From the series *Minjok kwa unmyŏng* [*The Nation and Destiny*], VHS (P'yŏngyang: Mokran Video, 1996).

6. Lee, "Early Twentieth-Century Poetry," p. 351.

7. Kim Ŏk, "Sowŏl ŭi ch'uŏk" [Remembrance of Sowŏl], *Chosŏn chungang ilbo* [*Chŏson Daily News*], January 14, 1935. For a translation, see "Afterword: Remembrance of Sowŏl."

8. Kim Sowŏl, "Chindallaekkot" [Azaleas], *Kaebyŏk*, July 1922, p. 7.

9. Sŏ Chŏngju, "Sowŏl si e issŏsŏ ŭi chŏnghan ŭi ch'ŏri" [Sowŏl's Poetry and the Treatment of Resentful Feeling], *Hyŏndae munhak* [*Modern Literature*], 1959, p. 571. For the list, see *Kim Sowŏl chŏnjip* [*Complete Works of Kim Sowŏl*], ed. Kim Yongjik (Seoul: Seoul National University Press, 2003), pp. 571–584.

10. Kim Sowŏl, "Pi onŭn nal" [Rainy Day], in *Kim Sowŏl chŏnjip*, pp. 404–405.

11. Arthur Symons, *Knave of Hearts: 1894–1908* (New York: John Lane, 1913), pp. 80–131.

12. Ŏm Hyŏngsŏp, ed., *Han'guk hyŏndae sisa charyo chipsŏng* [*Complete Collection of Korean Modern Poetry*], vol. 1 (Seoul: Taehaksa, 1982).

13. Kim Sowŏl, "Sihon" [The Soul of Poetry], *Kaebyŏk*, May 1925, pp. 11–17.

14. Maurice Berger, "Epilogue: The Modigliani Myth," in Mason Klein, ed., *Modigliani: Beyond the Myth* (New Haven, Conn.: Yale University Press, 2004), pp. 75–86.

15. Kyung Moon Hwang, "From the Dirt to Heaven: Northern Koreans in the Chosŏn and Early Modern Eras," *Harvard Journal of Asiatic Studies* 62, no. 1 (2002): 137.

16. Kim Dong Sung, *Selected Poems of Kim So Wol* (Seoul: Sung Moon Gak, 1965).

1. For My Love

Someday Long After

Visit me, someday long after,
and I might say *I have forgotten.*

Blame me, in your heart,
Missing you so, I have forgotten.

Still blame me for all of that,
Not believing you, I have forgotten.

Today, yesterday, I did not forget you,
but someday long after, *I have forgotten.*

Plucking Grass

Up on the hill behind our house the green grass grows,
and across the floor of the grove's sandy stream,
shadows of the grass I tossed in go floating away.

Where, I wonder, is the love I long for?
Every day, thoughts of my love return.
Every day alone on the hillside out back,
every day, I pluck grass to toss into the stream.

Tossed in, borne off on the stream's flowing waters,
as the grass blades float lightly away,
how the waves seem to press, nudging at my breast.

Where, I wonder, is the love I long for?
With no place to give my piteous heart rest,
every day I pluck and toss the grass on the water,
letting cares, like the grass, go floating lightly away.

The Sea

Where is the sea whose pulsing white waves
fall and rise as the seaweed grows red?

Where is the sea whose fishermen sit
on their boats as they sing songs of love?

Where is the sea whose sky cobalt hues
at twilight die gently away?

Where is the sea whose old wandering birds
build flocks as they follow away?

Where is the sea I long to cross over,
another land there on the far side?

On the Mountain

Up on the mountain, looking out
where the sea blocks the way,
before my eyes, floating in a dream, a dream of sky,
the village appears where my love now stays.

As idle boat songs drift in from afar
by the landing place crossing the white sands,
day turns dark, fog thickens and covers,
while the waves break into flowers falling far away.

Nightfall at last, the water birds cry,
the boats, one, then two, set out after the waves,
over the vast sea, the very sea,
and are gone like fallen leaves.

Alone on the mountain I keep watch the night through,
and as I drench my body in morning's red light,
I turn my ears to the water's faint song
passing the window where my love now stays.

Though at the swaying, waking song of the water
my love should startle awake and look out for me,
high up on the mountain, there on the mountain shall I be,
deep and fast asleep, and know nothing at all.

The Old Stories

As the dark night quietly draws on,
as night draws nearer the dim lamp's light,
alone in pain and solitude
I cry endless tears.

Before, I knew nothing of tears,
as I passed along this small stretch of life.
The old stories of long, long ago
I learned with no sense of their sorrows.

But now that my love has gone away,
gone and truly left me,
everything I had thought was mine
has slipped away, now is lost.

Only those stories I learned long ago,
those alone remain with me.
Growing day by day ever stronger, the old
stories bring me to helpless tears.

Love's Song

The clear song of my dear love
is always filling my heart.

Outside the gate I stand the day long to listen,
and my dear love's sweet songs
come to my ear as the sun goes down and all turns dark.
As night draws on and I fall asleep, they come.

Gently swayed in the song melodies
I enter deep into sleep.
I lie down alone in this sleeping place,
but still they comfort me as I enter deep into sleep.

But when I wake, my dear love's songs
have been lost and are gone with not a trace.
Try as I might to hear them again,
I have lost love's songs, with not a trace.

Untitled

Look, dear friends, the sun goes down,
sun goes down, and day passes by.
Quick now, put on your coats;
let us climb past the peak too.

Look, dear friends, the sun goes down.
Everywhere the world glitters, bright.
Little by little, it all turns dark.
Now we have the darkness, and night.

Look, dear friends, night comes on.
The bats rise up by our toes.
Enough, now, so close your eyes.
Then let us go back down the valley too.

Love's Words

Two months life flowed on like water,
stale water in the earthen pot leaked all away.
The words *I am going so let us go together*
are like an arrow piercing a living target.

The grasses may grow again in spring,
but like a tree broken off to its stump
or a bird that has broken both wings,
my body shall not flower again.

Each night, when cock's crow marks the first hour,
it is the time to go out to greet your spirit.
When the moon at month's end hangs at the ridge
is the time to prepare the rites for your soul.

Though life may flow by like water,
the words *I am going so let us go together*
might mean try to forget you,
but I shall never forget them till I die.

For My Love

It is not that I did not spend
many days till nights in thought of you,
while now the thought of you brings
but a dream by the damp pillow's edge.

In a strange place here by the town crossroad,
I have turned twenty just as the day turns sadly dark.
Though I might search the dark fields at night,
you stay my sadness forgotten.

Even now when I think of you
tears like rain by the sandy riverbank
are but a dream by the damp pillow's edge,
while you stay my sadness forgotten.

On a Dry Riverbank

Where frost struck leaves piled up,
traces of water still, underneath?
Moonlight weeping each night over the leaves,
a trace of waters that flowed away.

Sound of washing sticks, sound of water; songs of the
    nymphs in the fable.
Overgrown, the rock tops the waters once rushed over.
Dry field of reeds, pebbles overgrown,
where now the water's traces linger.

Sound of washing sticks, sound of water; songs of the
    nymphs in the fable.
Overgrown, the rock tops the waters once rushed over.

2. Spring Night

Spring Night

In dark tresses of the weeping willow's ancient limbs,
in vivid blue of the swallow wing blouse,
and there by the wine house window, just look. Hasn't spring
    settled in?

Silently the winds blow, weep, sigh,
while without a reason we know sadness and longing this
    dark spring night
as gentle vapors rise and cover the ground.

Night

Going to sleep alone is truly lonely.
Longing pierces the heart,
even while it seems your face,
your face may be utterly forgotten.

Now the sun has gone down and darkness gathers
round this place well known as Chemulp'o, in Inch'ŏn.
Darkness comes down slowly in the drizzling rain,
sea winds are shivering cold.

Yet as I lie down peacefully,
as I lie down in peace,
the high spring tide runs white
as all before my eyes is choked off by tears.

Long Ago in a Dream

Snow outside, only snow falls.
Moonlight, silent, enters by the window.
That woman who drew near with the dusk
enters my dream to hold and embrace me.

My pillow is drenched with tears,
for hasn't she just up and departed?
In the quiet dawn the figure of a single star
peers in through the crack in the window.

One Who Came in a Dream

So as I had become older
the one who always stayed hidden,
in my dreams, deep asleep, she came again,
her ruddy face, slender fingers just as before,
acting so unaware, lying down composed
in my arms, while still, still! Nothing,
nothing to say! Just that
silence. And just like that she rises up,
the sound of chickens fluttering their wings.
Wide awake in the brightness of day,
I go on mistaking
anyone on the roadside for her.

3. Two People

Snowy Evening

This evening as the wind dies,
as white snow comes pelting down,
just what you might be doing
this very evening, now this year . . .

Even a dream, just let me have one!
Falling asleep, won't we meet?
The one I lost, that very one,
she comes riding down the white snow.

Evening. Let the white snow come pelting down.

Purple Cloud

Beautifully colored deep purple cloud!
The skies are clearing.
Snow that fell unseen last night
has blossomed over the pine grove.

Morning sun glistens,
clumps of snow leaping.

What passed last night . . .
all forgotten, looking out.

Just the purple cloud stirring.

Two People

White snow one flake,
another,
then covering all the mountain peak.
Straw boots bound up, cotton leggings set,
knapsack tied tight,
even at a distance as I straighten and turn
she is still there,
she is still there.

Cock's Crow

It's that you are gone, why I keep
hearing the cock's crow rising in my heart.

As night turns deeper
and sleep more far away,

how hard it is to reach a dream.

Such the hurt,
but why is it so painful to live?

Where dawn shadows lie scattered, I walk
alone through the grassy fields.

Unforgettable

Unforgettable, that thought may come,
but as you pass on through your days,
as you live there will come a day you will forget.

Unforgettable, that thought may come,
and yet as life passes along,
though you would not forget, some things, some time,
    you may.

And still there is this other thing,
Longing so fondly I cannot forget,
will even that thought go by?

I Did Not Really Know Before

Spring or autumn, every night the moon rising,
I did not really know before.

To feel that longing pierce so deep,
I did not really know how before.

To look at the moon, even so bright,
I did not really know how before.

Just how that moon could be all sadness now,
I did not really know how before.

Sleeping or Waking, Sitting or Standing

Sleeping or waking, sitting or standing,
I had a friend with me always, like a shadow.

Ah, how much of a life we have wasted
spending it in useless regrets!

Today yet again, weeping for what I cannot ever know,
your heart, and you, I must shake myself loose and just go.

Empty intent, heart pained by restless bitterness,
must be what love is, or forget whatever it was.

Though the Sun Is Sinking at the Mountain Crest

Though the sun is sinking at the mountain crest,
it seems to be growing dark because of you.

Though the sun itself rises over the mountain ridge,
it seems that morning turns bright because of you.

Earth may collapse or the sky fall in,
but until the end, all that is, is because of you.

This is my only thought, that if the time should ever come,
like a shadow I will be with you.

Oh you, who once were my love!

4. No One Lone Mountain

Dream

Don't they say that dogs, roosters,
and other animals too have dreams?
Spring should be a time for dreams,
but I have not a one.
O the very end of my life!
I need a dream! I need a dream!

Day of Worries

On this day
you were to come you haven't!
This day of worries, fretting
as if you were coming!
All at once the sun is down,
and the day, dark.

Sky's Edge

Mine to all at once
leave the house,
scramble up the mountain
and be there looking down on the sea.
The boat is out, sailing the sky's edge.

Ant

When azaleas blossom
and winds noise about the willow's branches,
the ant works steadily,
narrow-waisted ant,
for half a spring day, all of today again,
steadily wearing itself out to build its house.

Swallow

Even the swallow flying back and forth through the skies
has its strong, familiar nest to come back to,
while I cannot but be sad, creature without a home.

Owl

Last night
outside the back window
an owl had come, crying,
while all day long the clouds over the sea were dark.
Today again, no sun seen, turns to night.

The Great Wall

Each night, every night,
on through the night,
I build up and break down
the Great Wall!

Buds

Though seeming less,
yet sufficient,
near springlike,
how the trees, all the branches, are now budding!

5. One Time, One Time

Cigarettes

My thoughts turn faithful to my cigarettes,
conspirator friends for that deep, long breath.
There was someone I met somewhere once
who told me they are the leaves that grew on the tomb
of a girl born and straightway seized by death
in a time now lost and long forgotten.
Listless, dull smoke drifts before me,
traces of a flame that lit, begins to fade away.
O, how my own heart torments me!
If only these long, desolately empty days
might be consumed as surely as you!

Untitled

This stream, that stream both dashing along,
but what, what does it mean?

You, whose heart knows nothing of faithfulness.

Deep gorge dark as death,
and you in my strangely unnerving dream,
a blue flame wavering,
your two hands reaching out at me.
Let them cool in the passing winds.

Bright full desolate moon,
in dawn's flowing waters' song
as if hiding in the cold, shyly,
here, as if in the water's bed.

You, whose heart knows nothing of faithfulness,

how this mountain and the next stand facing each other,
what would it mean at all, to you?

Mom and Dad

To live well or not is not the point,
just to be alive, not dead,
even about not being unable to die;
but this year with a son at fourteen, and daughter, both,
Sunbok's dad can't just end it, can he?

Parents

When the falling leaves drifted rustling down
the long winter eve,
sitting with Mother, the two of us,
I listened to the tales of long ago.

Was I somehow born just for this,
to be listener to such tales?
Foolish question. Someday
won't I be a parent and know?

Remarried

That woman left single
they say someday soon will remarry, she will.
And why ever not? Ten years ago that fellow
left her to live all alone; longer than together.
That's what life's all about, exactly that.

Lost Heart

All I seem to think of, wandering, weary,
in that far place so long gone from home!
And just as spring winds blow
and flowers bloom, why have you come here,
when I had almost managed to forget I knew you?
You, like some dream of long ago,
in my heart that knows no place to rest its sad coming and going.

Spring Rain

Flowers falling, expressionless, just falling the spring passes,
and rain falls, expressionless, the spring weeps.
Nothing in my heart but this sadness.
See, the greening branches, the clouds high up.
The day grows late and seems already turned to dusk.
Sad sweet rains come to a stop, but I
settle down to weep by the flower bed.

Silken Mists

When silken mists wrap snowy fields
is a moment never forgotten.
Met, and wept, on such a day,
that day of longing to madness was such a time.

When silken mists wrap snowy fields
is a time life alone cannot be endured.
It was then a young girl with her dress sash hanged herself
from a branch where buds were starting.

When silken mists wrap snowy fields
is the time when skylarks soar.
For the fields, for the sea, even from the skies,
intoxicated with all, and we don't know why.

When silken mists wrap snowy fields
is a time that can never be forgotten.
The time of first love was just such a day,
that day of parting will be forever such a time.

Memory

Under the moon, she was standing, expressionless,
that woman standing, her pale face,
her face, pale, a bit of faint color in the cheek.
Under threadlike, spreading branches
her black hair gleaming.
The chill night river waters
rush past P'yŏngyang Fortress's walls.
Woman, the way you were standing there, expressionless!

You were close that one night I longed for,
and in a deep dream, for a time you
gave our bodies to the weeping,
turning heartsick longing to love.
Just outside the wall, the alleyway quiet
as April turns, a sleepless night
keeps one or two lamps dimly shining:
Woman, the way you were standing there, expressionless!

Impatient Love

Why don't you come?
Moonlight in the window, the plum blossoms'
shadows shifting shake my heart.
O, just let me close my eyes now and sleep!

Somewhere distant, something, a sound
of the spring season's tides
in the Land of Waters, Nine-Storied Palace, deep inside
    the Palace Brilliant,
where the dragon princess, sleepless—song, dance,
    the sound of the water
in the spring season.

Every dark corner in my heart . . .
In a perfectly clear mirror, a place locked in spring's clouds,
a whispering rain falls, the moon wreathed in its dim halo.
Why don't you come right now? Why won't you come?

Terrible Dream

Woke up from a terrible dream
at daybreak, in spring.
Ravens, magpies screeching, their disturbing noise.
What was it that appeared before their eyes?

Lovely spring daybreak, the grasses drenched with dew,
the whole world calm, at peace,
yet the ravens out there, and the magpies screeching:
Was it that my awful dream visited them too?

While the spring winds pass quietly over the empty fields,
and on the eastern hills flower petals scatter,
hear how this woman worried by love has determined
everything is an omen meaning her ill.

Dream Visit

Deep in the night
a lamp glows dim red.

A footstep
just heard, then not . . .
The sound of a step dies away.

Though she turns and turns,
once lost, sleep is gone, won't return.

Deep in the night
the lamp glows dim red.

Woman's Scent

The scent of the moon wearing clothes of pale clouds.
Scent of the sun wearing scarlet clouds.
Not that, but sweat scent, scent of stained clothes,
scent of skin and clothes wet with rain.

The pale sea . . . boat rocking . . .
A breath soft, longing;
her faint, small
cries, bodies together . . .

The scent now of a grove a small death has passed.
Scent of a small boat rocked like a seesaw.
Scent of the sea and the fish.
Scent of lying prostrate under the sky in sudden spring heat.

Winds sweep down over the dunes and blow the fog away,
and moonlit evening cries out faint as lights in the distance.
Full of scent, how good her body was!
How good it was, her body, scent-full!

Powdered Face

Face very pale, reflecting the dim firelight,
that face giving off a lonely scent;
cup that came and went, taken, given to lips;
slender hand reaching nearer, then away.

Heavy and dark as it all was, still reddish;
and vague, indistinct, yet clear:
the song sung to a *kayagŭm*,
or as moonlight flowing above the wood.

You it was, and I, and that woman,
three people at night, three and the night,
as the long spring night above the wine cup
and outside the window, once again sank silently toward the dawn.

l. 7 A *kayagŭm* is a zitherlike stringed instrument.

Wife's Body

On the swelling tides, there is the place
the boat must have started from.
You, sweet other to a wife now,
Truly, before they all are crying Mama, Mama.

Smoke escapes the chimney crack
and an itch that starts in what's not hard as a rock.
You, clear as sky, young as young,
For kindness such as yours, the way to heaven is clear.

Seoul Night

Red light.
Green light.
Green light for the open road.
Red light for the dead-end alley.
Electric lights are flashing.
Electric lights flicker.
Electric lights dim.
Electric lights guard the night with their lives.

Deep in my heart,
in a secret place bright and dark,
red light cries out in tears,
green light cries out in tears.

Red light.
Green light.
The far distant night skies are jet-black.
The far distant night skies are jet-black.

How we like the streets of Seoul!
How the Seoul nights please us!
Red light.
Green light.
In my heart's secret place
Green light is lonely,
Red light is lonely.

6. Half-Moon

Autumn Morning

Ash-gray, rooftops glisten
beneath the pale blue sky,
winds moan as they come and go
among the grove's sparse trees,
while the mountain village, seen, then not,
is wrapped in fog.

Dawn, a cold rain.
The stream freezes under leaves.
Wrapped in tears, all memories
bleed like a new wound,
cry like a newborn infant,
surrounding my soul with their whispering.

*Wasn't there a day your heart felt easier
in its longing for that one time?*
Ah, how that dear voice goes on
whispering, soothing,
till at that voice I forget hatred, forget shame,
and weep, endlessly, without rest.

Autumn Evening

Waters white and farther than heaven,
clouds redder than the sun.
How sad, as I wander the far plain,
weeping, thinking of you.

Ahead, shadows deepening,
the endless path reaches on.
Under tall trees, the river village
seems to rise into the sparse branches.

But no one promised to come!
There is no one I should wait for.
Yet still I am here, walking the pond's edge
as twilight steadily fades over the water.

Half-Moon

When did it rise, the dim half-moon,
over the sky, climbing pale?
A wind rises, evening is cold,
and the sun sinks into the clear waves.

Dark, and darker, the grassless fields,
where a cold fog rises and hovers over.
Ah, the winter turns deep, and in my body
this grief keeps pressing down on my heart.

Love gone away, taking even the love from the heart,
until youthfulness has turned to old age.
Branches of the field brambles, dark with night,
let their leaves fall, petals pale in the evening light.

7. The Cricket

This Thought of Meeting

Evening sun has faded down a dim road,
distant mountains draw clouds down into darkness.
What brings even now this thought of meeting,
when my love has no way to find me?
For whom do my aimless steps hurry?
The moon rises, wild geese call in the sky.

Familiar Faces

At the end of thinking comes the drowsiness,
at the end of longing, to forget.
Say nothing at all, from now, and we will know
nothing of that sadness of knowing no familiar faces.

Deeply Held Belief

Deeply held belief, the words in my empty heart,
when I see the two, three, or four good friends who stop only
    to go:
Before long, you'll see I have no more use for you!

Dream

Dream? Spirit's uncovering. Sorrow's home.
Cry, my love, for flowers falling, and spring growing dark.

Sweethearts and Friends

In sadness a friend is welcome,
but in love, a sweetheart is better.
Tonight as pepper pods ripen
and strawberry flowers blossom and scent,
you sing! Let me drink.

Paper Kite

The sun settles on the afternoon crossroads,
the town's streets wear an early winter loneliness.
As I lean absently in the doorway
a paper kite, like a white snowflake, sails away!

Falling Snow

Pure white over the ground, snow is falling.
Through a day of waiting, snow is falling.
This day he has not come again, snow is falling.
Each time I light the evening lamp, snow is falling.

Lump of Grief

Kneel, rise, incense candle lighted.
In my heart, small lump of grief.
In shadows of the fifth-day moon, rainwater weeps.
In my heart, small lump of grief.

Optimism

In living, must be determined
on just this sort of life,
just this sort of life
where winds cry in branches bare of flower and leaf.

Wind and Spring

Wind blowing in spring, windy spring,
spring winds blowing, shaking the sparse branches,
winds that shake my heart blowing spring,
This spring! This wind! In my body
it all cries out *Flower! A cup of wine!*

Snow

White as snow white, light to step on snow,
light as ashes flying up falling down snow,
blown away by the wind, snow melting only in flame,
that woman's heart, my love's heart.

Pledge Deep as Deep

When starting up from a bad dream, I lie back down;
when mountain plants poke up now spring has come;
when some handsome youth passes ahead of me:
all bring back to mind what I
near forgot, *that pledge, deep as deep can be.*

Red Tide

Running before the wind, that red tide,
each time that red tide runs in,
I would climb up on that wind,
robe myself in blue-green clouds,
and holding that fiery sun close,
together with that red tide
leap up, leap up and play with that red tide.

Some Other Country's Land

Steel bridge, as I look back it's
over there I rushed across in confusion
steady my breath, now my feet planted
on some other country's land.

Thousand, Ten Thousand *Ri*

I am determined, unstoppable,
body-flinging-down determined
on this thousand, ten thousand *ri* I shall go.
Leap quick as an arrow up
this road and go, and let
the burning mountain, the mountain burning
raise its columns of smoke, one, then two!

Life and Death

Lived or died says the same,
since living, a person grows older and dies.
But if this is so true of life, why should I feel it so
again today, at the very top of the mountain
I climbed to stand, weeping?

Fisherman

How pleasant, to live knowing nothing of how it all falls apart.
Today from the fishing village the other side,
one fishing boat set out again, it is said,
no matter how terrifying the waves last year too.

Cricket

Sound of mountain winds,
sound of cold rains falling.
On a night you talk of life's changes,
the fire at the country tavern dies down, a cricket cries.

Moon Color

Bright moonlight, a cricket cried,
night you held me briefly, thoughts gone blank,
O why on this night can't I find you once again
and take you away to Seoul?

8. If the Seacoast Changed to a Mulberry Grove

If It Wasn't for Bad Luck . . .

As you weep at your misfortune, I know
what turned your luck bad,
blew it away in a passing wind,
carried it off in the tides,
all the way down to your heart's hard core.
As if it were any of it my work.
All over again, and yet again
the reddish waves pounding into your heart,
the dark green lichens
growing by the rough rocks
at the water's edge.

If the Seacoast Changed to a Mulberry Grove

Sorrow mine, such as cannot be ended,
darkening spring night, petals passing on,
the passing petals fluttering.
Now, what they might say
is the sea has changed to a mulberry grove.
So it is, this lovely time of spring,
fresh, as all things become strange to the eye,
their appearances unfamiliar,
yet so sad, don't you see? So sad,
even spring, the days of March past,
red as blood rising up and falling,
those petals, there, far off, those petals.

Wax Candle Lamp

Quiet night, not a voice, white
outside as the wax candle leans by the clear window,
guttering down into dark and goes out.
I wonder, here alone, at my face in the mirror,
no point or purpose to it.
And it occurs to me: *We*
spend our first night in a dream;
death comes while we sleep,
and we just go out, not a decent thing to show for it.

Should We Just Say Whatever Words Are in Our Minds

Complaining, appealing, heave a sigh,
all you who find life so hard to bear.
Trying the refined, the elegant phrase,
all the most sophisticated of this world, listen, you!
Should we just say whatever words are in our minds?
To consider twice, then thrice, before,
can only be the start of a losing proposition.
It is one of life's rules, not to know;
another's miseries, one does not comprehend.
Do not speak of life, the world, people,
a good name in the world, the fine words to say,
for just to strip another of his clothes
and leave him standing at the street corner
is just to leave a devil post to look at.
From this day forward, O people
of the world, set your ransom
at the cheapest price you can bear
and then go on.
If only that could be so, from now on,
and heaven be honored, no matter how sad, afflicted,
how solitary we might be.

A Later Day

What father and mother said you know
by heart, how *Raising sons or daughters,*
means looking forward
to the days to come.
Just so. And clearly,
all were born of two parents.
But my friend, what does this mean?
What will be taught, hands raised,
long from now by a generation
who grew up all together and learned it?
Never mind the days to come,
but raise sons and daughters
with a true heart until you grow old.

Man and Wife

O my wife, my love!
As heaven-made partners,
don't you believe we were perfectly meant?
So is it true still or not?
Strange, unfathomable human mind,
always asking, *Is it true or a lie?*
How could any estrangement sever
two bodies woven together in affection?
A life, said to be half a hundred years,
if we are lucky enough to live it!
So what is the length of the marriage tie?
Just let me say, whatever else may happen,
when we die let us be buried in one tomb.

My House

At the base of a distant hill, the edge of a field,
hard by the shore of the broad sea,
I shall build it, my own house,
and put a wide road out front.
Those who go by, some
might stop in, then go on alone.
The day will turn dark at the rise by the white rapids.
I shall stand at the gate and wait.
From shadows growing lighter as dawn birds cry,
the day turns bright and still,
the morning comes sparkling,
and I look at each one who passes, wondering
Might it be you? Might it be?

Dawn

Fallen leaves hiding my feet,
I stood alone by the pool's edge
before a tall tree's dim reflection,
the eastern sky still dark, dark still.
The heavenly one's tears of love
became clouds that flowed down
over my lonely dream's pillow. And yet—

And yet, my love, come quickly as a cloud
that has climbed the east, glowing red, faintly red,
is fixed at the sky's midpoint
while the old half-moon fades into gray.

Cloud

If I could ride that cloud,
that cloud dyed blood red,
dark cloud, dark at night,
I would climb up on that cloud
and ride through the skies,
all ninety thousand *ri*,
to be wrapped in your embrace as you sleep.
Alas, it cannot be! So listen to me, love:
When that cloud turns to rain
and tumbles down to you,
just think, my tears, each night.

9. Summer's Moon

Summer's Moon

This night of the cool bright moon,
summer night hazy with clouds,
the fresh, drenching, red dew falls
from unbounded, solemn skies.

Among the highest branches
young insects, happy spirits,
creep through the leaves' cool shadows—
Ah, such waves of gladness!

Branching, spreading, ascending,
even thorn vines are bathed
in the moon's oil-like vapor.
Ah, such beauty exiles sleep!

As curving grass stems dance
and the rushes sing their soft song,
O shape into words the ages
held in the light sifting down!

The houses are quiet with sleep
as the wind from the fields of rice
leaves a fragrance consoling
like silver through the village.

The farmer who worked all day,
now as the father, peacefully sleeps.
Hoe and rake alone reflect the light
from dim shadows at the thatch edge.

As cicadas gather their voices
crowding through the night, in the field
a farm woman's shadow
lingers still by the well's edge.

As moonlight fades, withdraws,
clear stars emerge from the deep sky.
From the cicada's cry, music flows—
Ah, the happiness of a summer night!

Beneath the leaves this cool summer night,
memories filled with the burning passions
of youth in a farm cottage
hover in the faint moonlight.

Can we who once had much pride
find again in this life, in this world,
a time better than this moon night,
than summer spent in a farm village?

Set worrisome trifles down.
Listening in the midst of the stillness,
set oar to the moon's golden waves
and open your voice to the night-blue sky.

Ah, praise it! That once we knew
the joys of life ever flowing.
This night of the dim, summer moon,
tears fall of gladness like a dream.

Approach of Spring

Thoughts of the spring days coming
put to an end this long, desolate winter.
Today on the aspen's outstretched limb
a white bird, not there before, perches singing.

Still, by the snow-covered mound
is it a shadow, fog, some trick of air?
Here and there gathered beneath the peaceful sky,
villages rest, motionless.

A band of magpies chatters aimlessly.
Staring at the sea, a raven cries.
Somewhere with gong and chanting
sounds the young child's funeral dirge.

This time, the wanderer, hesitant,
knows not where his steps may lead.
Though piercing tears fall without end,
in the skies, behold life's peace.

Unable to draw near or to go,
in lonely doubting confined,
this day we each have lost our love
and mourn that none could keep her heart.

Waiting to approach, in the ache of thin fingertips
spring sends its voice.
In forest depths, paths tangled as hair
wind fretful about the legs at each step.

Water Plants

Flocks of birds, hungry, making their noise
in branches of a dried-out tree at sunset.
Stream that ran all day exhausts itself
where at sunset the valley's throat is blocked.

Who should know the worn-out traveler
who climbed the lonely valley
where a single cloud is caught
had tasted all the bitter, all the sweet?

Where is the place where General Nami
led his horse to drink the water,
now flowing again, overflowing the banks
of the Tuman River, one hundred, one thousand *ri* along?

Is this not the high hill of Musan?
From ages past, those who fought for justice
and lost must hide themselves, try to disappear
like good-for-nothing fellows.

Who could imagine that another would rise up,
grasping a sword, driven by three hundred years

l. 9 General Nami (1441–1468) led forces suppressing a rebellion in the north.
l. 17 "Another" may well refer to Hong Kyŏngnae (1780–1812), who led a
   rebellion in the north.

of resentment, of disgrace
far beyond human power to endure?

But one there was, who made of split bamboo
a bow, sword from a rusted hoe,
and raised the flag of justice high,
banging on the drum the length and breadth of the land.

Who will recall the uproar at Tabuk Village,
the clothes bloodstained,
anxious hearts turned to coal in one night
beneath the moon sinking down at Chŏngju Fortress?

Morning dew on the water plants,
flowers that bloomed on the burning mountain,
I look up now and cry out the name struck still
at not fulfilling what was to be fulfilled.

---

l. 11 "Morning Dew" happens to be the title of the song "Ach'im isul," by
    Kim Min'gi, which became the unofficial anthem of the student protest
    movement of the 1970s.

10. Forsaken

Our House

There is no one who would pass through
this lonely spot, so I settled in,
thinking *I'll spend one night and go on.*

As a song comes
from a boat setting out
there, at the western edge of the sky,

tears fall from eyes softly closing.

Our house stays clear before me,
whether I am dreaming or awake.
Over that mountain and over the next,
still the clouds flow on.

Picnic

Field flowers
bloom
and scatter.

Field grasses everywhere
grown thick and tall,
while a snake's shabby covering
shakes apart in passing gusts.

See there, how everywhere, everything
glistens, alive!
Spreading its wings,
the swallowtail kite flies high.

At times I go
only to stop once again,
my heart
refreshed to overflowing with this joy.

And my steps, again, still before me . . .

Forsaken

In a dream I cried out
awakened
and came out to the field.

In the field,
a gentle misting rain,
frogs croaking in the deepening shadows.

I hesitate, hands clasped behind me,
nervously scanning the ground.

From within the firefly-swarming forest
someone calls, *I am going, stay well,*
and sings.

Solemnity

I climbed up onto the burial mound.
In the spreading light of the morning sun,
as grasses and leaves were gleaming
the winds whispered.
But
O, my wounded heart,
my body shakes quietly with the pain of it,
now at this very moment to feel full well
the weight of that solemnity humans bear.

Only Think, If We Had Our Land, Our Own to Plow

I dreamed
that shoulder to shoulder with my companions
I was returning to the village after a full day of work,
in the evening light, happy, in such a dream.

But I have lost my home.
Only think, if we had our land, our own to plow!
Instead we wander at evening, and in the morning
earn newer sighs, new lamentations.

South or north, or east,
my body floats away, just look at it,
the shining of hope, the faraway distances the stars light.
Waves rise, against the bosom, legs, and arms.

And yet this overwhelming sense of favor,
that day follows day before me
as the path, barely discernible, still goes on. And I
go on, a step, one more. Just visible, on the mountainside
are companions, there, or there, alone, doing the plowing,
and the work of weeding.

By the Furrow

The two of us
sitting by the furrow, the field full of tall, ripe barley.
O the joy of resting from work done,
as now in our conversation, our words bloom like flowers.

Sing, then, how as the sun comes down
the flocks of birds sing their glad songs.
Such blessings, such blessings fill all living things to
    overflowing.
Earnest thanks, let the thought be deep in our hearts.

What is life's purpose? Loving heaven covers all,
so the two of us, we two can work, and while we live,
look out on heaven and earth, day following day,
feeling the new and renewing joy, always on this same land.

With a renewed laugh we stand, the two of us,
starting back through fields the winds dance through.
As we grasp the hoes, all is in order, all as it was meant,
in our joyful setting forth, the very purpose of life.

Evening

Horse, cattle, herds and groups all have gone back,
the empty fields filled only with the sound of frogs croaking.
Clear skies descend even lower, distant mountains and passes
    dark;
and nesting birds have all returned to the tall trees to roost.

Far and wide, the fields,
as I stare out upon reflections off the water,
standing as if transfixed, low on the hill,
and breathe a deep sigh, though why so?

Put it out of mind, and from this point on into the night
my body grows light in my thoughts, my spirits rise ever
    higher.
Suddenly I can see through the reeds, not far away,
the stars have risen, and their light!

Hands Together

A visit, just the two of us. Night's lights sink down upon us.
Just look, where the moon works its way in among the trees.
We walk along in conversation where the wind stirs.

Streets are quiet under the lamps. Toward the west,
shadows, still, as if aglow,
while closer, the dew on the fields glistens.

Night deepens, all four directions turning still,
while right here, no more words, no more walking,
lost by the roadside, we stand eyes closed, facing each other.

From far away, a mountain temple bell sounds.
    The moon is setting.

Meditation

Deepest night, night's spirits chill,
straddling the window sill, my legs dangling,
I hear frogs croaking.
How sad, that you went first and now are sleeping by
    yourself.

I am still, thoughts and body. Through the trees,
indistinct, lights pass by, a family's ceremonial procession.
After a time, the voices of the frogs and the prayers have all
    faded away.
My spirit overflowing! . . . into the space between heaven
    and earth.

Quietly I rise and cross over, settling close by your sleeping
    form.
No movement, none; all sounds and voices stilled.
Lights of the stars silently glancing down
tell my body *Here, even closer, infinitely closer.*

11. Alone

Delight

Heaven choked, dark and deep,
a glimpse of a ghost
emerging from the depths of a dream.
Bands of rain lashing down,
strands in the willow tree black with shadows.
The sounds of the spell, the incantation bending away.

Letting her black hair loose,
dear daughter has started away, wailing loud.
Insects, shells cast off, squirm and wriggle.
The sea dark as blood, while at the hole
in a dead tree the woodpecker
hammers away, keeps hammering away.

Grave

Someone calling me, the sound
here and there on the red hill
the tombstones moving in the moonlight,
while the song, the voice left of it, falls down around
where all records of the ancestors lie buried.
I look everywhere,
but only the traceless song settles over,
while here, and there on the shadowy hill
the voice of someone who seems to be calling me,
the voice calling, the calling voice
trying to seize my soul and tear it out of me.

Prayerful Spirit

In this prayerful spirit I meant to share,
until I tied up everything in one bundle and started off
that morning, along the red line of the dew-wet rocks,
staring at the sun as it rose, my mouth open wide.

How you do wander, O my prayerful spirit, like the gull,
the tomb alone, heaven glistening above, the clouds;
all there was in life lost at the seashore,
and after this body is dead and gone, what could be done
vanished too!

Or my prayerful spirit, above the mountains shabbily
    clothed,
the stream of smoke rising from the fallen leaves,
evening blown in the winds, scattered spider webs,
the dew formed at night will fall again.

In this prayerful spirit, meant to be together,
in life that was once and is gone,
only as day follows the one before and they vanish with the
    cock's crow,
so close, only you who were so close to me, be so once again!

Cold Evening

Faint, bluish moon
hangs itself dimly in the gaps and spaces
in the fallen-down walls of the old village shrine,
while a pair of ravens spread their wings against the wind.

Clustered, the grave mounds seem to shudder,
the base of the red hill emerges from the melting snow,
until here it is, streetlights off at a distance,
the house I would have built, and entered, O my heart!

Life again more distant than the tomb,
tears no warmer than water.
O my heart, a bonfire leaps up,
my whole life, autumn passing, in our yard.

Still I would rather I heard
that voice, the snowmelt soaking
the earth, as each night I look up,
the moon hung on the corner of the wall as I look up.

Invocation

O name broken in pieces!
O name dispersed into the emptiness!
O name I call that no one owns!
O name that I will die calling!

Even at the last I could not say
the one word left in my heart.
O you that I loved!
O you that I loved!

The red sun is caught on the mountain ridge.
A herd of deer cry sorrowfully.
On the mountain where it stops, about to fall,
I call out your name.

In grief overwhelming I call.
In grief overwhelming I call.
Though my cry goes bending away,
the space between sky and earth is too vast.

Even turned to stone where I stand on this spot,
O name that I will die calling!
O you that I loved!
O you that I loved!

12. Loneliness of the Journey

Loneliness of the Journey 1

June, dusk, strands of rain,
like the bones of a corpse wrapped up,
carried floating, sinking, soaking on a coffin plank,
    the wayfarer
without destination, still at this red door.

Loneliness of the Journey 2

The sea that I long for even today,
the thought of seeing it again overwhelms me with tears.
Your kindness, the light touch of your hand, like powder,
surrounds me still, causes me to tremble
like the aspen leaves, as I think of the sun rising
over the sea, there where I was born
and grew up, my home.

13. Azaleas

Song of the Stream

If you had been born as a wind!
In the middle of an empty field by the stream at moonrise
you would blow loose all the ties of my clothes.

Or if we had been born as wriggling white bugs!
We would try dreaming that foolish dream
of a rainy black night at the foot of some hill.

If only you had been born as a rock on a cliff
where the sea comes to its end,
the two of us would embrace and tumble in.

Let my body be the spirit of fire
burning in your heart the night through,
the two of us burn to ash and vanish.

Road

Again last night
at a wayside inn,
ravens crying *kawak, kawak,* awake all night.

Today,
how many miles
again lead where?

Up into the mountains,
down to the plains?
With no place that calls me I go nowhere.

No need to speak of my home,
Kwaksan in Chŏngju,
that the train and the boat go there.

Hear me, wild geese
in the sky,
is there a road in the air you travel so sure?

Hear me, wild geese
in the sky,
I am standing at the center of this crossroads.

Again and again the paths branch,
but not one way
is mine.

Stream

For what reason
do you act that way?
Staying on alone by the stream

when green grass shoots
push their way up
and wavelets ruffle up in the spring wind,

I think over your promise,
that *going away*
is not really going.

Each day coming out
to sit by the inlet,
I keep turning it over in my mind.

Going away
is not really going.
Isn't that your asking me not to forget?

Road Away

I miss you.
But should I say it,
I would only miss you more.

Should I
leave without a word,
once again?

Ravens on the mountain, in the fields,
and as the sun sinks lower on the western hills,
they cry.

River waters flowing, tumbling
down say *Come down, come*
follow away, and still
they go on, flowing away.

Wangsimni

Rain is falling
falling still,
the falling rain,
and if it fell five days, let it fall!

The eighth day or twentieth,
you said you would come when the tide ran full,
and then on the first or fifteenth, you would go.
Go, and go on for another ten *ri* it is raining.

Whatever for, that bird
must cry and cry so
go on your way, another ten *ri* and cry away, cry away.
Worn down by the rains, the field bird cries.

Willow trees by Ch'ŏnan Crossing
soaked and drooping, let down their strands.
Though the rain falls a full five days, let it fall!
Caught at the ridge peak, even the clouds are weeping.

Mandarin Duck Pillow

Clenched teeth grind
at thoughts of death.
Moonlight dapples
the window edge.

Tears, curled in sleep
on the bent arm pillow.
Spring pheasant, sleepless,
comes and cries in the night.

Mandarin duck pillow,
where is it kept?
On the pillow where two once slept
wasn't the vow made *While we live, till we die?*

At the foot of the spring hill
a cuckoo cries,
cries out
My love, my love.

Mandarin duck pillow,
where is it kept?
Moonlight dapples
the window edge.

Detachment

This spring coming,
three years since coming in marriage,
has come to a wild, empty plain.

Flowers on this wild, empty plain
bloom after dying, true.
Two, now three years
waiting without news.

The river that flowed straight, they say
since last spring has bent an arc and flowed back,
but don't talk of how, over the rapids below,
the water's color stays green as ever.

Three years since coming in marriage,
and always
the flooded inlet waters have flowed on
past the wild, empty plain.

Mountain

Above on a black alder tree
a mountain bird cries.
Why does it cry, the bird? Deep mountain gorge,
it cries trying to cross over that ridge.

And the snows fall, and falling, cover over.
Today again, on a day's journey
of seventy, eighty *ri*,
turned round, trying to make just sixty.

No way back, no way back, still no way back,
to Samsu Kapsan there is no way back.
A man's heart might let some things go,
but full fifteen years, a love cannot be forgotten.

In the mountains, falling snow, and on the fields, the snow melting.
Above on a black alder tree
a mountain bird cries.
The road to Samsu's Kap Mountain is a ridge road.

Azaleas

When you turn away from seeing me
and go,
gently, without a word, I shall send you away.

From Mount Yak in Yŏngbyŏn,
azaleas
I shall gather an armful and scatter them on your way.

Step after step away
on those flowers placed
before you, press deep, step lightly, and go.

When you turn away from seeing me
and go,
though I die, no, not a single tear shall fall.

Sakchu Kusŏng

Three days by water, three by boat,
a long three thousand *ri*,
and by foot still another three thousand *ri*:
Sakchu Kusŏng is six thousand *ri* over the mountains.

Even the swallows, drenched in the wet,
try but turn back, beaten by the rains.
At evening, the mountains looming,
and at night, the mountains loom.

Over the mountains, Sakchu Kusŏng,
a long six thousand *ri* away.
At times, sometimes in dreams, four, five thousand *ri*
the path runs out and back, out and back.

Apart, one heart longs for the other,
longs for the place where love stays.
Can't you see, even the birds long for home
as they come and go, back and forth, north and south?

Clouds adrift at the end of the plains,
just where would they be going at night?
Over the mountains, Sakchu Kusŏng
lies a long six thousand *ri* away.

Seesaw

The young girls of Sŏngch'on
leap high in their game of seesaw.
Eighth of April, Buddha's birthday,
so they leap to the seesaw.

But O, the winds blow,
how the winds blow!
Do not set the double swing
with elegantly ribboned lines,
there beneath the weeping willow
within the walls.

Where willow limbs reach down outside,
outside the walls,
willow limbs reach over and down—
O my, dear sister!
Where willow limbs descend so prettily,
how deep those shadows are!

Overwhelmed by a spring day
so good as this,
for the young girls of Sŏngch'on
the seesaw is a practice of love.

Ch'unhyang and Yi Toryŏng

The Taedong River in P'yŏngyang
of all the streams in our land
flows the most beautifully, we know.

And there at the midpoint of three thousand *ri*
traveling the length of our land,
lofty Mount Samgak leaps up.

How right it is, my sister, O my sister!
that long ago and faithful to our land,
lived Ch'unhyang, they tell of, and her Yi Toryŏng.

On this side is Hamyang, on the other, Tamyang,
where sometimes in a dream crossing the mountain
the Magpie Bridge might be found, if you try.

How right it is, my sister, O my sister!
Where the sun and moon rise, in the land of Namwŏn town
lived the virtuous maiden, Ch'unhyang.

l. 9 Ch'unhyang and Yi Toryŏng are heroine and hero of the narrative love
story "The Tale of Ch'unhyang." A recent movie by the director
Im Kwon-taek brought the story and the *p'ansori* narrative performance
style to an international audience.

Cuckoo

Cuckoo,
　Cuckoo,
My little brothers, *Cuckoo*:

Our sister who lived by the Chindu River
comes to the village by the Chindu
and cries.

Long ago, far away
in our land,
our sister who lived by the Chindu River
was killed by her stepmother's jealousy.

Call out, *Sister!*
O, the sadness!
Our sister who died by a stepmother's jealousy
died and became the cuckoo.

Never forgetting, not ever forgetting
the nine younger brothers left behind,
when the night is dark, at the third hour
when others all are sleeping, moving
from mountain to mountain
she sadly cries.

Thought of Home

From high on the mountain
look out at the sea:
The four directions, a hundred *ri* or more,
and rocked on the great waves
a ferryboat setting out.

Where but here is the great temple on the famous mountain?
In the incense burner and on table, the broad brass plate,
the evening sun as it crosses the mountain peak,
while in all four directions a hundred *ri*, just the sound of the
    water.

Pray let me return home again in glory, while I am still young,
on a flower-fine day like this one, in splendid robes.
But the ferry set out, tossed and rocked.
How could I go, a hundred *ri* or more in all directions?

A hen pheasant cares for her chicks in the mountains,
but I am here, ten thousand *ri* from nowhere.
Looking out from deep in these mountains, throat tight,
all before me is a blur of tears.

If I go back down to the flats
and look carefully back,
at the ridge where fair sun and moon take their ease,
clouds now just wander, layering up and up.

Flowers of the Mountain

On the mountain flowers bloom
the flowers bloom
autumn spring and summer through
the flowers bloom.

On the mountain
on the mountain
the flowers blooming
all alone there the flowers bloom.

Little bird that sings on the mountain
fond of the flowers
lives
away on the mountain.

On the mountain flowers falling
the flowers fall
autumn spring and summer through
the flowers fall.

14. Lighting the Flower Lamp at Night

Lighting the Flower Lamp at Night

Night. Lighting the flower lamp, might meet in the deep
    back room.
Still too young to know, all they think,
Mind's bright as the sun and the moon, up to anything.
But no, love is not just once or twice, though they do not
    know it yet.

Night. Lighting the flower lamp, meeting beneath the dimly
    lighted window.
A body that still doesn't know the way ahead, what's to
    come, they all think,
Mind's as firm as bamboo or pine, up to anything.
But no, life is a thing of frequent tears, though they do not
    know it yet.

Riches and Honor, Wealth and Fame

That face, mine, in the mirror, facing me,
had I only known it better sooner than now.
That people live unmindful the day
they grow older is the day they die;
and even if this were true, still,
where has my life been?
Sixteen would be a good year from this moment on.
Could I at such an age again
be more than before, a bit more,
I might know better that living at all is living.
That face, mine, in the mirror, facing me,
had I only known it better sooner than now.

Repentance

The effort of life, even for some no-good thing,
were he doing some good work;
but how vain even to think of it.
And I know, when we cross
over the hill at last, for the horse
at some country inn, in the setting sun,
there is that moment of quiet dozing,
having carried the weight, by the stable,
that moment of quiet dozing.

Insincerity

I know how you want to ask about thinking it over again,
with, *What exactly was it you could not believe*,
but today, this moment,
its cruelty invisible to our eyes,
what use is it to say a heart
like water has flowed away and vanished?

Black clouds that linger at the base of the hill,
mountain deer calling so piteously,
I would bring them to my heart and embrace them.
But the tide falls, night grows dark,
no way to know where the anchor was let go.
Only the trade on the streets of the town,
all done on credit, the letting and the getting.

Dream Path

Spring, dawn, bead of water, distant roads
Between fields and sky, the broad forest groves
Scent drenched, red leaves above it, the road
Cold chilling wind reflecting drenched wet grove
For me, what is to be walked, the road
Wrapped in evening shadows, and night's, your dream
Above the bridge, shaking, the rainbow's road
Fall and spring, wild and rough as the winds dream

Human Beings Live to Die

How many times in a day do I wonder,
I wonder, is there something I have been living for?
I have lived not knowing, but know
that the stream which flows on
flows on to end in the sea.
So it is, it might be said, which means
forget all this giving it a try.
Human beings live to die, it is true;
but I shall be like the ant
building its house
in the spring-warmed earth.
I shall live like that, like
that while I live, until the day,
rejoicing in life,
for if living is the purpose of being human,
then there is no need to strive again
since human beings live to die.

Right to Seek to Die

Nothing more to hope for, truly,
the light, or is it empty sky?
For my song, only a voice left to it,
I can send flying off into the wind.
Not having done what I tried, is it right
to seek to die, to have seen from a slightly higher place?

To live an entire life
and just disappear after living it,
I know well is true, having lived
till now, having come to this.
Of all that I have gone through till now,
if only I might say I have lived and reached it!

Oyster shells scattered at the water's edge;
an old red thorn, spreading;
a day that grows gradually darker and darker;
a pile of stones wailing in the windy rain:
I keep watch over the quiet night, late, wondering
is it right to seek to die, not having finished what I tried?

Hope

The day grows dark, snow falls,
and I have come to this unfamiliar shore.
A mountain owl cries,
fallen leaves spread out beneath the snow.

O landscape, lonely and bleak,
I have earned these tears of knowledge!
If only I had known before!
Everything in life
is but a lovely
shadow in the corner of the eye.

Autumn night, and a deep fragrance
as everything is withering.
Shadows of trees huddling together
over the fallen leaves, wind and rain crying . . .

Panoramic

Lowering skies, even day itself not yet light,
dawn, white snow that has settled on valleys and rises,
while off to the south above the water's edge
strange clouds rise close and thick.

The village children
have climbed in a bunch to the schoolhouse,
while young married women from time to time
come down to the spring.

Waiting by the railing, looking out alone,
I see the whole morning, my heart
as if a painted scene had been set inside,
all at once blurring in hot tears.

The huntsman, gun over his shoulder,
wind blowing his hair, half white,
sets off at a run. He has come all the way.
A morning when white snow covers every hill and valley.

I Have Lived Not Knowing Life at All

Going, and won't be back, such words
rattled round useless in my ear.
Up past Mansu Mountain,
a love who long ago broke away,
if only I could see her once again today.

I have lived not knowing life at all.
With the lips of one worn down by better and worse,
I might have said the very same
words, slightly more cleverly.
If only I had lived not knowing life at all!

Don't we know what they mean, the words
It's so cold, when you turn your back.
The fires burning on Chesŏk Mountain,
if only they were the grasses burning
on the tomb of a love who long ago broke away.

15. Golden Meadow

Golden Meadow

Meadow
meadow
golden meadow:
Deep, deep in the mountains burns a fire,
the golden meadow round my love's tomb.
Spring has come, spring's light has come,
even to the tips of the willow's threadlike branches.
Spring's light has come, the day of spring has come
deep, deep in the mountains to the golden meadow.

River Village

Day darkens. In the rising moon
white waters flowing ceaselessly,
golden sands sparkling . . .
Carried away on the young mule, O my husband!
Here, the river village,
village where I am left to live alone.
As late spring is past, I too,
even I mourn for the family.
Some man of virtue, looking for a place to stay
as the day turns dark,
and someone, widowed in a river village.

First Skirt

Spring departing, day ending,
flowers falling as spring grows dark,
and helplessly I weep for the falling flowers,
helplessly sense the spring departing.
Holding a bare branch, its flowers fallen,
I weep as if mad, married away from home,
as light fades, spring comes to an end,
and round my waist the new skirt
is drenched with tears,
while I weep helplessly for the falling flowers,
helpless as I sense the spring departing.

New Moon Celebration

Celebrating the full moon on the moon's new year,
let us all go out together and celebrate the new year's moon.
Putting on our new clothes,
leaving sorrows of the heart where they were,
let us all go out together to celebrate the new year's moon.
Friends and neighbors, off to see the new year's moon!
When the moon climbs over the mountain and out onto the
    water's surface,
we shall go back together, neighbors and friends.
When the three gold evening stars begin to fall,
let us go, all together to celebrate the moon.
By the tomb of the friend who once went with us,
celebration of the full moon on the moon's new year.

O Mother, O Sister

O Mother, O Sister, let us live by the river.
Where golden sands glitter in the garden,
and beyond the back gate, the reeds are singing . . .
O Mother, O Sister, let us live by the river.

16. Rooster Cock-a-Doodle-Doo

Rooster Cock-a-Doodle-Doo

Cock-a-Doodle-Doo, the rooster crows,
but my arms embraced nobody at all.
A long night filled with wrenching worries;
dreams broken open, eyes tight shut but sleep will not return.

Above, the grass-green hill on Misty Isle,
    above the Taedong River,
last night moored at Namp'o.
Get up, turn, lie back down in the boat,
shutting the eyes tight but still the longing comes.

No matter how you look for it,
the red lamp light is so faint.
Close the eyes, a white sandy plain appears
as the mist rising over the sand vanishes above the waters.

The sun rises over the Taedong ferry crossing.

REMEMBRANCE OF SOWŎL

Kim Ŏk

Sowŏl is gone, so whatever I may say here can be nothing more than the memories of a time that is now past. He was a poet who stood at the height of his youthful powers, one who had shown great talent, and yet like a whirlwind in the depths of night, a dark fate has plucked him away. This is why I feel such sorrow at the loss of Mr. Kim Chŏngsik, a poet of great promise.

No one will deny that it is human nature to love life and to abhor death. How much greater must our sorrow be, then, when a person of talent dies before having had a real chance to show it? It is for this reason that we feel such deep regret in our hearts at Sowŏl's untimely death. Yet life and death are a part of humanity's unavoidable condition. There is no way to deny it; no matter how much strength one possesses, one can only bow the head in acknowledgment of this firm reality.

Where can my thoughts turn, after all, on this day when a poet is gone for whom so much had been expected? Should I think back on the lines of the poem by W. B. Yeats, and sigh in agreement that "All that's beautiful drifts away / Like the waters"?[1] If not, should I then wander in the evening by the side of a darkening tomb, chanting some sad song? And if not, then what? One cannot hold on forever to the gentle memory of a time that will not return.

The heartless months go by, night and day taking their memories with them. They escape. And a person's mind, too, is like flowing water. It is a cloud drifting in the bright sky. Water and cloud, in the mornings one winds round the base

of a hill, and in the evening, the other wanders restlessly in
the northern sky. The mind is a thing that changes with time
and place, so no matter how deeply we may feel something,
that feeling cannot be preserved forever. Even in sorrow,
there is no escape from forgetting. Some person might be
babbling in a completely drunken stupor, and yet there will
surely be an awakening; and awake, all that has gone before
will seem like a cloud that floated away without a trace. How
can one assert that a promise made in the full brightness of
the moon never, never to forget, that even such a promise will
indeed last?

Filled as they now are with sorrow at Sowŏl's untimely
death, with the passing of a day or two, my thoughts will be-
gin to lose him. This adds to my sense of regret today. Even as
I recall the Sowŏl of a time now past, I feel remorse at my own
ungrateful heart. All the more so because Sowŏl was someone
who had few friends in the literary world. Although one can
find traces in his poems of this unhappy poet's loving pres-
ence, other remembrances of him as a man or friend are scarce.
I cannot help but think, now, of a song that Sowŏl wrote early
in his life. Titled "Unforgettable," it declares that no matter
how hard one tries not to forget, in time there will come the
day of forgetting.

Unforgettable

Unforgettable, that thought may come,
but as you pass on through your days,
as you live there will come a day you will forget.

Unforgettable, that thought may come,
and yet as life passes along,
though you would not forget, some things, some time,
    you may.

And still there is this other thing,
Longing so fondly I cannot forget,
will even that thought go by?

Sowŏl seems to have spoken of himself in this song. In the
months that sneak by, a person will one by one lose track of
memories. And if separation in life is sad, how much more so
is the separation of death? When I hear of the sadness of death,
I think of Sowŏl and the unbearable sense of loss, as in Sowŏl's
own song:

I Did Not Really Know Before

Spring or autumn, every night the moon rising,
I did not really know before.

To feel that longing pierce so deep,
I did not really know how before.

To look at the moon, even so bright,
I did not really know how before.

Just how that moon could be all sadness now,
I did not really know how before.

Now that the author of this poem has been lost, it causes
me to think of him. I return with that poem to a past that
seems so very distant, and I try to find expression for my bitter
feelings in supplication. Doesn't this poem, too, seem like some
unexpected presage of his fate? How can I avoid my thoughts'
turning dark, as I think back on this poem and the time when
Sowŏl was just eighteen or nineteen years old, a time when he
and I would meet almost every day to talk about the poets of
the East and West and their works?

I must speak of Sowŏl even as my faltering memories of him
grow every day more faint. What were this poet's attitudes
about poetry? What was his life? As I consider these ques-
tions in turn, at the same time I lament this unhappy poet's
untimely death.

If it is possible to know and understand an individual's pri-
vate life—the personality, interests, thoughts—the likeliest

way to try to do so is through that person's private letters.
When that correspondence happens to have been addressed to
a friend, it is all the more likely. In order to reveal more fully
the nature of Sowŏl's personality, I shall make public a letter
that he sent to me not very long ago. I cannot help but feel
that it wrongs Sowŏl in some way to do this, but there really
is no alternative. I believe that the poet might have forgiven
my indiscretion.

One year ago, I sent to Sowŏl a copy of my book of trans-
lations *The Daylily*. His letter came in reply. I should note
that in the last three or four years since his path and mine
had separated, our exchange of letters had declined to only
one or two in a year. And in addition, I should note that be-
tween us there remained some of the formalities of the student–
teacher relationship.

He wrote:

> I am deeply moved, after these several years, to receive a
> letter in your hand. As I open and look through the book
> you sent me, straightway there appears before me a vision
> of that time, now long past, when I was studying with
> you. I wonder if the lilies of the title are the daylilies that
> forget anxiety. Are they the lilies of forgetting? To my
> way of thinking, it would have been good to name my
> mind after the daylilies that forget so easily.

So he wrote, and I might venture here to guess the outline
of his feelings at that time. I realize that he was referring to
anxieties that cannot be forgotten precisely because they are
so keenly regretted. There were many anxieties on his mind,
anxieties that he regretted. He went on:

> Next year will be the tenth since I came to Kusŏng.
> Somehow these ten years have not seemed to be a short
> time at all. Sanch'on has stayed much the same since I
> came here; and my dealings with people have become
> rather few. The world seems to have abandoned me,
> and I live all alone, as if in escape. I don't write. I don't

study. I don't do any work. I just seem to let slip from
my hands the bits of money that were so hard to gather.
I am now out of money again, and wondering what I
should do.

The poet had tried many different kinds of work, all of
which ended in failure. Here he is looking at that desolate,
cruel reality. His words make me feel the deep, unshakable
melancholy too. He had lost everything, and was looking
back unhappily at his own shadow. He continued:

> In the recent issue of *Samch'ŏlli* magazine, the following
> Chinese quatrain appeared:
>
>> One part of life is a floating cloud rising;
>> of death, one part is a floating cloud vanishing.
>> The floating cloud itself has no essential form.
>> So too with life and with death.
>
> This is what I think. The person who quoted these lines,
> saying "Don't worry, don't worry" at a conference on the
> Mortality of Man's Fate, as much as replied "I don't
> know" to the question of what is human nature. For my
> part, if what I happened to be saying after a few cups of
> wine made no sense at all, I would be quiet, and do
> whatever I felt like by myself.

So he wrote, and we can infer what his thoughts were.
Again he took up his brush to continue. Since it was the time of
the harvest moon, he had many feelings of remembrance.

> From olden times it has been called the Mid-Autumn
> Festival. Tonight the moonlight outside the window is the
> moonlight of an old romance when the woman is leaning
> against the bridge railing, weeping bitter tears as she is
> drawn from her cruel fate by thoughts of death; that
> moonlight, bright and cruel as the light of day. Today
> being the fourteenth, I plan to return tomorrow to my

home in Osan and, for the first time in ten years, pay my respects at the ancestral tombs.

He goes on:

They say that autumn is a sad season for patriots. Does that make me a patriot? Soon I will put aside my hempen clothes, and dressed in cotton stand at the edge of a field of withered grasses that have been bent down by the winds blowing these many days. As I stand there, my mind sorrows for the time I once lived so rough and brash, a time from which I am now quite estranged.

So saying, Sowŏl turned with a sorrowful look back to the time when he had been filled with great enthusiasm for writing, though he later came to set his brush aside. Moreover, since he as much as said in this letter that he would write again, it does seem that one way or another his thoughts were returning to the composition of verse. But then I think of how he was taken away before bringing out any of those compositions. It is an awful loss.

Sowŏl wrote in closing:

I will read the book you sent to me, not forgetting even though its title and you as well tell me to forget. Setting aside any discussion as to the merits of the work, or whether the collection is made up of translations or your own work, I look forward to reading it whenever the time gets long; or when I lack a drinking companion because my purse is empty; or when dreams are hard to reach in my lonely bed. In closing, I append a poem I have just written. Its title is "Replying to Ansŏ's 'Samsu Kapsan.'"[2]

Sowŏl thus for the last time sent me a poem. Though he wrote it without premonition, and though I read it the same way, thinking now of how it was to become his posthumous work, I am overcome by the sense of deprivation.

What brought me to Samsu Kapsan?
Here, the wild peaks,
waters tumbling down, the steeps
piled up! Alas,
what place is this
Samsu Kapsan?

Longing for my home
I cannot return.
Samsu Kapsan is so far, so far!
That ancient road to exile
leads here!

What place is Samsu Kapsan?
I have come here, but cannot return.
No way back! If only
I were a bird I could go free.

I cannot go, cannot go
back to the home where my love stays.
To come, or to go: the thought mocks me!
Alas, Samsu Kapsan imprisons me.

I long for home, but Samsu Kapsan
is my prison.
No way back. For this body
there is no escape
from Samsu Kapsan.

As I now make this letter and the poem public, I do feel
some easing of my mind. It may be a discourtesy to the poet
who has passed away so abruptly; but if they were not pub-
lished now, they would be lost and forgotten as time went
by. I am reminded here of one of Sowŏl's earliest pieces.
Titled "Someday Long After," it tells us that even if one
tries not to forget, there will come a time when all memory
will have vanished.

Visit me, someday long after,
and I might say *I have forgotten*.

Blame me, in your heart,
Missing you so, I have forgotten.

Still blame me for all of that,
Not believing you, I have forgotten.

Today, yesterday, I did not forget you,
but someday long after, *I have forgotten*.

Such, then, is the human mind. One tries not to forget.
One tells oneself that the loving memories held gently in the
heart can be brought back at any time. But can the skies pre-
serve a constant brightness while the winds blow and the
clouds roll by?

Sowŏl was not someone who was dominated by emotions.
Rather, he was someone in whom intellect won out over feel-
ings. He was what I might call a tough-minded person, some-
one who did not shy away from calculating his own interests
in any given situation. I do not mean to say that other factors
were not involved, but in his decision to give up writing, he
was persuaded by the realization that there was no living to be
made from poetry.

When Sowŏl went to Tokyo to study, his decision to en-
ter the commercial program rather than a department of
literature was another instance of his rationalistic approach
to life.[3] However his feelings might have been inclined,
whatever the possibilities in a given situation might be, if
he could not give it his careful consideration, there was but
one conclusion: the poet would give it up with a shake of
his head.

He possessed a rather severe integrity, and having such in-
tegrity, he could be quite unforgiving if he discovered that
somebody else had made a mistake. He was uncompromising,
in a word; an individual who could not accept easy alterna-

tives. The same disappointments that others might have borne gently, he encountered with a bitter sadness. What appears in the poems he wrote after his twentieth year is that kind of sadness. Such a person may well possess the strength and determination of self-control, but at the expense of the refinement that poets are conventionally thought to possess. When he was twenty, while his thoughts were not yet fixed and his experiences were few, for a time his expressions of sentiment were as bountiful as flowers in full bloom. There was a gentle softness and sentimental youthfulness in his writings then, as in his "Love's Song":

The clear song of my dear love
is always filling my heart.

Outside the gate I stand the day long to listen,
and my dear love's sweet songs
come to my ear as the sun goes down and all turns dark.
As night draws on and I fall asleep, they come.

Gently swayed in the song melodies
I enter deep into sleep.
I lie down alone in this sleeping place,
but still they comfort me as I enter deep into sleep.

But when I wake, my dear love's songs
have been lost and are gone with not a trace.
Try as I might to hear them again,
I have lost love's songs, with not a trace.

This poem is such a gentle, mysterious song of such quiet, inner purity. Sowŏl's original and lasting achievement, arrived at quite outside the influences of the contemporary poetical world, was just this kind of expression. At the time, everyone else in the literary world was ignoring the Korean language in an enthusiasm for foreign styles of expression. Sowŏl alone made use of the purest Korean language to give expression to his own, living sentiments. No other poet of the time comes near measuring up to Sowŏl on this point. One cannot help being amazed at such mastery of expression in the Korean language at that time.

Sowŏl exerted extraordinary efforts in revising his poems. Far from quickly dashing something off, he proceeded always with the greatest caution, multiplying erasures and corrections, corrections and erasures.

To give new life to the rhythm of his poetry, Sowŏl experimented with the line breaks. Even when he used the traditional seven–five pattern of syllables, rather than just writing out the usual lines, he would break off the line one way, or set one another way.

> *kŭripta*
> *mar ŭl halkka*
> *hani kŭriwŏ*

> *kŭnyang kalkka*
> *kŭraedo*
> *tasi to hanbŏn*

> (I miss you.
> But should I say it,
> I would only miss you more.

> Should I
> leave without a word,
> once again?)

The above are two stanzas of Sowŏl's "Road Away." For the stanzas to reach their present form required a corresponding amount of effort, for even after the words and the various revisions in their form had been completed, their original arrangement on the page was quite different from what it is now.

> *kŭripta mar ŭl halkka hani kŭriwŏ*
> *kŭnyang kalkka kŭraedo tasi to hanbŏn*

In order to enhance the original seven–five meter of the couplet, he divided it into the two stanzas as first given above. Anyone who reads the poem cannot fail to sense the distinctive beauty of rhythm that resulted from the poet's rearrangement of the lines. One might say that his attentiveness extended even to the rhythm of breathing.

If we add the next two stanzas:

chŏ sanedo kkamagwi, tŭr e kkamagwi
sŏsan enŭn hae chindago
chijŏgwemnida

ap' gangmul, twit kangmul
hŭrŭnŭn mur ŭn
ŏsŏ ttara orago ttara kajago
hŭllŏdo yŏndara hŭrŭptidaryŏ

(Ravens on the mountain, in the fields,
and as the sun sinks lower on the western hills,
they cry.

River waters flowing, tumbling
down say *Come down, come*
follow away, and still
they go on, flowing away.)

Although the meter continues to follow the same seven–five pattern of syllable counting, the rhythmic effect is quite different with this division and arrangement of the lines. While conditions may be different now, at the time when Sowŏl wrote this poem, not many years had passed since the entrance into Korea of what was called the "new poetry." Few poets at that time gave much thought at all, to say nothing of such meticulous attention, to the matter of phrasing and rhythm. There is no other poet who thought as Sowŏl did. However it happened, he was the one who helped to revive the use of our language. It is tragic to consider how much richer our poetic inheritance might have been if he had not abandoned his writing in midcareer.

If it is possible to divide Sowŏl's works into two categories, making a formal distinction between the folk song and the poem, clearly his skill lay on the side of the former. This is not to say that Sowŏl did not produce poems other than in the folk-song style; but in comparison, they seem rather formal products of the intellect.

> At the base of a distant hill, the edge of a field,
> hard by the shore of the broad sea,
> I shall build it, my own house,
> and put a wide road out front.
> Those who go by, some
> might stop in, then go on alone.
> The day will turn dark at the rise by the white rapids.
> I shall stand at the gate and wait.
> From shadows growing lighter as dawn birds cry,
> the day turns bright and still,
> the morning comes sparkling,
> and I look at each one who passes, wondering
> Might it be you? Might it be?

This is his poem "My House." Compared with any of his folk songs, it lacks their youthful brightness. Sowŏl hated to be called a folk-song poet, for whatever reason, and demanded that as a poet he be called a poet. Yet assuredly his skill is in a class by itself when he is compared with any other poet in the folk-song style. This will be easily seen by anyone who looks through his collected works, *Azaleas*. I will quote here one of his early songs, "Cuckoo."

Cuckoo

Cuckoo,
  Cuckoo,
My little brothers, *Cuckoo*:

Our sister who lived by the Chindu River
comes to the village by the Chindu
and cries.

Long ago, far away
in our land,
our sister who lived by the Chindu River
was killed by her stepmother's jealousy.

Call out, *Sister!*
O, the sadness!
Our sister who died by a stepmother's jealousy
died and became the cuckoo.

Never forgetting, not ever forgetting
the nine younger brothers left behind,
when the night is dark, at the third hour
when others all are sleeping, moving
from mountain to mountain
she sadly cries.

I need hardly point out that this composition is assembled
from the poetic elements of legend. At the same time that we
acknowledge the poet's concern with diction, we must also rec-
ognize his deep concern with the beauty of the rhythm. To the
extent that these concerns were consistent, it might seem that
the writer's poetic qualities were brought into full growth.

I shall not quote another of his very best poems, at this
point; but let us ask how the poet approached the matter of
diction and meter in terms of expression. No doubt every
reader is familiar with the famous "Azaleas" or his "Sakchu
Kusŏng." There are surely a number of Sowŏl's works that
will be favorites in the folk tradition for a long time to come.
In this perspective, again we can see that the world of poetry
has lost a poet who will be highly esteemed. Several years ago,
our friend Wŏl T'an praised Sowŏl's songs very highly in the
journal *Kaebyŏk*, saying they had appeared in an otherwise col-
orless literary world.[4] Wŏl T'an's remarks were by no means

meant as a eulogy at the time, but now that Sowŏl has passed on, the comments, too, have come to be a reflection of the past. As such traces disappear, memory is all that will remain.

> Is it easy to meet
> a friend on the road the first day?
> Go on a ways. Then meeting
> makes a friend on the road.

This is the first stanza of the unfortunate poet's "Pillowing Arm Song." If Wŏl T'an had by chance seen the poem, it is not difficult to imagine what he would have said. Because the poem is so long, I shall not quote it here. It is a song about a summer night's dream, about sadness. I don't really know if Sowŏl actually experienced it. That feeling of pathos, at any rate, is truly touching.

> And today for the night
> the pillowing arm of heartbreak.
> Tomorrow, the kŏmun'go[5]
> pillow of love.

So he wrote; or as follows:

> O friend who picked mushrooms
> in the pine grove on the hill behind the house:
> Into whose family, into what other home
> did you go to get married and live?

And so on. This does not seem to be just some literary amusement. If one reads the song in its entirety, one cannot avoid being struck by the sorrowful regret, so deeply felt.

Furthermore, the sad resentment and loneliness that appear in Sowŏl's poems were likely his own character. It seems that however things went, such deep despair must have remained the one constant and unavoidable element in Sowŏl's life. Whether he could not perhaps grasp the purpose of the poet's calling, lost as he was in misfortune, he at last abandoned it entirely. Having failed in business, having lost the stability of his livelihood, the poet's sense of isolation became immense. In his anger at such a luckless life, he would sometimes lose his normal capacity for intelligent, rational judgment.

In general, there are many good pieces among the works from the time when he was twenty or so; and the secure intelligence visible in the works even after that time was undoubtedly Sowŏl's own character.

One has to say that all of this has been the result of precocity. And in any event, the shortness of a life of just thirty-three years is most unfortunate.[6] This misfortune, for this poet, causes regret and sorrow that are unending. When I think of what he said about life and death, rather than his early death having been the consequence of what was some form of arthritis,[7] one must conclude that there is some new meaning to the term "premature death." Now that this day has come, alone as I am, I cannot help but reflect on how strange it is that Sowŏl's own attitude regarding life and death always seemed so thoroughly confident, without the least sign of fear or dread.

I have so many recollections of this unfortunate poet, recollections that make up my stumbling path toward him. But for now, I shall close with what I have written thus far, with the thought in mind that I shall write again at the next opportunity, quietly hoping, as the pitiful thoughts well up within me, that this unfortunate poet, Kim Sowŏl, may find peaceful repose.

I am saddened at the thought that I now confront, in my sorrowful reflections, what has become the literary legacy this poet has left to us all.

Notes

Kim Ŏk was Sowŏl's teacher at the Osan Middle School near P'yŏngyang and at the Paejae Academy in Seoul, as well as his literary mentor. This is a slightly shortened translation of Kim Ŏk, "Sowŏl ŭi ch'uŏk" [Remembrance of Sowŏl], *Chosŏn chungang ilbo* [*Chosŏn Daily News*], January 14, 1935.

1. W. B. Yeats, "The Old Men Admiring Themselves in the Water," in *The Collected Works of W. B. Yeats*, vol. 2, *The Poems*, ed. Richard J. Finneran, rev. 2nd ed. (New York: Scribner, 1996), p. 82.

2. Ansŏ was Kim Ŏk's literary sobriquet.

3. David R. McCann, "Korea the Colony and the Poet Sowŏl," in Marlene J. Mayo and J. Thomas Rimer, eds., *War, Occupation, and Creativity: Japan and East Asia, 1920–1960* (Honolulu: University of Hawai'i Press, 2001), esp. pp. 46–48.

4. Wŏl T'an's comment appeared not in *Kaebyŏk (Creation)*, but in "Mundan illyŏn ch'uŏk hamyŏ" [Recalling the Literary World's Year], *Ch'angjo* [*Creation*], January 1923. For Wŏl T'an's comment, see O Saeyŏng, *Kim Sowŏl, kŭ salm kwa munhak* [*Kim Sowŏl, His Life and Literature*] (Seoul: Seoul National University Press, 2000), p. 27.

5. A *kŏmun'go* is a zitherlike instrument.

6. Sowŏl was thirty-three years old according to the Korean calculation of age, which considers a child to be one year old when he or she is born.

7. Kim Ŏk called the illness "much mulberry disease" (*chŏda pyŏng*), a new coinage, perhaps meant to suggest the victim's trembling limbs. My thanks to Professor Song-Hun Kim for the idea.

CPSIA information can be obtained
at www.ICGtesting.com
Printed in the USA
JSHW031005110321
12421JS00008B/24